LEADERSHIP METAPHOR EXPLORER

Creative Conversations for Better Leadership

Facilitator's Guide

Charles J. Palus and David Magellan Horth
Center for Creative Leadership

CCL Stock No. PM004B

ISBN 978-1-60491-142-8

©2014 Center for Creative Leadership

Published by Center for Creative Leadership

Sylvester Taylor, Director of Assessments, Tools, and Publications

Peter Scisco, Manager, Publication Development

Kelly Lombardino, Manager, Global Publication Dissemination and Licensing

Stephen Rush, Editor

Karen Lewis, Editor

Layout by Joanne Ferguson

Acknowledgments

Many colleagues have contributed to the development of Leadership Metaphor Explorer as it has moved from an idea through several prototypes. Many thanks to Rich Hughes, André Martin, Steadman Harrison, Lyndon Rego, Bruce Flye, Greg Laskow, Clemson Turregano, Bill Adams, Jim Myracle, Tom Hickok, TZiPi Radonsky, Marie van Vuuren, Sarah Miller, Joel Wright, John McGuire, Gary Rhodes, Bill Pasmore, Diane Reinhold, Michelle Crouch, Barak Karabin, and Hamish Taylor.

Quick Guide

Leadership Metaphor Explorer enables creative, insightful conversations in and among groups of people about three topics: the kinds of leadership those groups presently have or practice, the kinds of leadership they need in the future, and how to develop those required forms of leadership—personally as one's own leadership style and collectively as a shared leadership culture.

Leadership Metaphor Explorer is a tool rather than a scripted exercise, and CCL recommends practicing first with just yourself and one other person. Each of the 83 cards illustrates a metaphor showing one of the ways people think about leadership.

The following is a typical way to use the tool, requiring roughly 30 to 90 minutes.

Prepare: Think about the purpose of the session. Get the right people in the room. Gather people together in small groups of no more than eight and no

This is flexible. We did it with 724. See pg 10.

fewer than two. Your session could occur during a regular group meeting, coaching session, program, class, retreat, and so on.

Frame: Ask the group to think about its big challenge (using its own words) and the kinds of leadership required to meet the challenge. There are many possible themes related to groups, leadership, culture, vision, strategy, beliefs, behaviors, boundaries, and so on. Spend some time in advance thinking about how best to frame this conversation for this group of people.

Browse: You can spread out a single deck for everyone in the group to see, or you can give each person in the group a deck to choose from. Each person chooses two cards, one for each framing question. The cards people choose represent their responses or answers to the questions. Typical framing questions include the following:

- Card #1: What is leadership typically like now in our organization as we face this challenge? (What is our leadership culture?)
- Card #2: What will leadership need to be like in the future to resolve this challenge? (What kind of leadership culture will we need?)

Reflect and Converse: Ask members of the group to discuss the cards they selected. Typical reflection questions the group members might use with one another include the following:

- Why did you choose each card? What does the metaphor mean to you?
- How are your cards similar to or different from my cards? Why?
- How do you interpret this card that I picked? What does it mean to you? What else could it mean?
- What patterns do we see across all the cards we chose? How do we interpret those patterns?
- What do I or we need to stop doing? Start doing? Continue?

Extend: Continue and deepen the conversation, if possible. Compare notes with groups having similar conversations. Begin to plan the leadership development that will be required for the future state. Preserve the cards (or digital photos of the cards) online and in digital reports, along with descriptive text, photos, and action plans from the conversations.

Contents

Introduction

Leadership Metaphor Explorer is a compact tool for enabling creative, insightful conversations within and among groups of people about three topics:

- the kinds of leadership they presently have or practice
- the kinds of leadership they need in the future
- how to develop the required forms of leadership, as individuals and as a group, organization, community, or society

The tool itself is a deck of 83 cards, each with a different metaphor (in the form of a drawing and label) for how leadership can be enacted. Leadership Metaphor Explorer is playful as well as serious, and deepens dialogue in an engaging way. You can find a more detailed explanation of the ideas and the work underlying the tool in *The Leader's Edge* (Palus & Horth, 2002).

The Leadership Metaphor Explorer cards are available in digital form for use in slide shows, creative digital media, and other kinds of reports and presentations. To see the digital version, go to www.cclexplorer.org/metaphor.

What Is Leadership Metaphor Explorer?

CCL finds it useful to define leadership in terms of its outcomes: direction, alignment, and commitment. Leadership happens among people with shared work, in the interactions that create direction, alignment, and commitment (McCauley, 2011).

Each card represents a way of thinking about direction, alignment, and commitment in the context of leading organizations, teams, or other social groups. The cards are effective in helping people have conversations about the kinds of leadership they have and the kinds of leadership they need.

Leadership Metaphor Explorer is a result of CCL research that studies the forms of leadership needed in an increasingly complex and interdependent world (McCauley et al., 2008; McGuire & Rhodes, 2009; Palus & Horth, 2002).

6

IN-THE-MOMENT COACHING

Our CCL colleague Clemson Turregano did an impromptu coaching session with his client, a CEO, with a set of Leadership Metaphor Explorer images Clemson had stored on his iPod Touch.

I was showing Leadership Metaphor Explorer on my iPod to JB, the CEO of Big Co., India Division, while we were waiting in the lobby of a hotel. We did an impromptu one-on-one coaching session. I handed him the iPod and showed him how to browse the digital Leadership Metaphor Explorer. He said he liked the tool, and then I casually asked him, "Where are you now, as a company?"

He chose the one labeled Ruthless Gang Bosses, laughed, and said, "Gang of idiots—that's us."

We talked about that awhile, and then I asked him, "Where do you want to go?" JB said that the people who reported to him had a lot of autonomy and big egos, all of them had different agendas, and the team was all over the place in terms of what it wanted to accomplish. He wanted the team aligned and focused on one objective. He picked Squadron of Jet Fighters and talked about ways in which he and his team could all be flying together in sync.

What Does Leadership Metaphor Explorer Do?

Leadership Metaphor Explorer helps people think more clearly, collaboratively, and strategically about leadership, which creates the potential for people to take more effective actions in response to complex challenges. The tool draws attention to any or all of four levels of leadership, all of which are necessary for developing more interdependent forms of leadership (Palus, McGuire, & Ernst, 2011):

- society
- organization
- group
- individual

In particular, Leadership Metaphor Explorer helps people understand the leadership culture in which they live and work. The leadership culture of any collective is the constellation of deeply held beliefs and related practices that shape direction, alignment, and commitment (Drath, Palus, & McGuire, 2010).

In a business context, Leadership Metaphor Explorer helps an organization address important questions about its business strategy and its leadership strategy (McGuire & Rhodes, 2009; Pasmore & Lafferty, 2009):

- How well do the organization's current leadership culture and subcultures support our business strategy?
- How can we adapt or transform the organization's leadership culture to support its business strategy and meet the challenges it faces? What are the broader social contexts and scenarios that demand consideration?
- What is the organization's leadership strategy for enabling its business strategy?
- How does my own individual approach to leadership align with the organization's leadership strategy? How might I adapt my approach for a better fit?

Further, Leadership Metaphor Explorer helps people think about the following:

- their own actions and beliefs about being leaders and the available alternatives
- options for facing and resolving complex challenges
- leading a group by defining how it wants to accomplish its work
- leadership cultures and subcultures within organizations
- leadership for community engagement and social change
- leadership for spanning group, organizational, and cultural boundaries
- leadership strategy for long-term success
- the kind of leadership needed to meet their organization's current and future mission and vision, and how to develop strategies for meeting the challenges that making those changes will bring
- how to develop more effective leaders and more effective leadership
- leadership as the social processes from which emerge shared direction, alignment, and commitment
- leadership outcomes at the levels of society, organization, group, and individual
- the types of leadership culture as revealed in CCL's extensive work with organizations, groups, and individual leaders: dependent, independent, and interdependent (also seen as developmental stages for transforming organizations)
- how to generate more open and honest conversation about leadership in their organizations or communities

Using Leadership Metaphor Explorer

Leadership Metaphor Explorer can be used in any number of ways and with all kinds of people. Although it's most commonly applied in small groups of leaders who use it to talk about their work and their future development, there are few limits to its use.

Later in this guide we present a number of applications and examples at societal, organizational, group, and individual levels. Before we go there, let's review some of the possibilities when you consider the size of the group, the audience of which it's composed, and the global reach of today's working groups.

Group size. Leadership Metaphor Explorer can be used with a group of any size. It's useful for individual self-reflection, for looking at one's own leadership approach, or for trying to understand someone else's perspective. As a one-on-one coaching tool, Leadership Metaphor Explorer can work as a conversation starter and help people open up with their intuitions and emotions. Leadership Metaphor Explorer can be used as a dialogue tool for small groups, in intact teams, in breakout groups at a conference, and in classroom groups. Leadership Metaphor Explorer can also be used with large groups at presentations, in auditoriums, and at conferences.

Audience. Leadership Metaphor Explorer is adaptable to almost any type of audience. The tool can be used in schools, programs, camps, and retreats to help young people thinking about the different ways that people work together and relate to others. The frame for using the cards doesn't have to be explicitly about leadership. For a younger group, you might frame the session as People I Like to Be Around and then move into topics of responsibility, authority, trust, collaboration, and so on.

We've used Leadership Metaphor Explorer as a research tool in microfinance and small-business banking programs in India and Africa to understand the organizational cultures they want to create.

—*Lyndon Rego, director, Leadership Beyond Boundaries, CCL*

Designer's Tip

Try these exercises if you use Leadership Metaphor Explorer with a large group.

1. For a Leadership Metaphor Explorer session at a conference, give each person an envelope with three random cards. Ask attendees to share cards with each other and respond to the session's framing question. Follow up the responses by dividing attendees into pairs and asking them to talk to one another about their responses.

2. Randomly assign a card to each person in the session, and ask him or her to relate it to a question chosen from a list of general questions that you have prepared beforehand (for example, How does the card relate to your vision? When are you most creative? When are you at your best? When are you at your worst?). As an alternative to questions, you can ask the people in the session to respond to a simple statement or give them directions for making a response (for example, Use your assigned card to tell a story about leadership where you work).

3. Break the session group into small groups, and then gather the favorite images and themes of each small group into an overall profile. It often happens that different groups consistently choose the same cards in response to the framing question.

With a more traditional audience, Leadership Metaphor Explorer proves quite effective in helping people address issues of leadership culture and leadership talent in relation to business strategy, and we have used it in business contexts ranging from executive boardrooms to MBA classrooms to work teams. Leadership Metaphor Explorer has also been useful in exploring and crossing boundaries in organizations, including the boundaries between different leadership subcultures that one finds in different functions and geographical regions. Likewise, Leadership

Metaphor Explorer has been successfully used in government and military leadership contexts (Hughes, Palus, Ernst, Houston, & McGuire, 2011).

We are often asked whether the cards are serious enough for serious people. Do the drawings, the card format, or the metaphors detract from their appeal? Our experience says no. Senior executives and military commanders tell us that they find the cards appealing or at least acceptable. After a serious and frank conversation gets under way and the cards are working, senior business and military leaders like them even more.

Global reach. Leadership Metaphor Explorer has been used successfully all around the world. The metaphors represent a range of global contexts, even though they are inescapably tilted toward American and

Figure 1. Leadership Metaphor Explorer was used in Iraq to help U.S. State Department and Defense Department leaders and staff to reach across the boundaries that define their missions and their work.

Designer's Tip

Many of the cards have been deliberately created to have a negative connotation. In some environments or cultures, they might get in the way of a productive conversation. Even those not deliberately created this way may feel negative to you. Feel free to remove cards from the deck.

English language origins and the metaphors those languages make available. It's always a good idea for a manager who plans to use the Leadership Metaphor Explorer cards to scan the deck and remove (or be prepared to explain) any cards that might be confusing or controversial for a non-American audience. (See What Do the Metaphors Mean? on pages 79–85 for a brief description of each metaphor.) Managers should encourage participants to locate the discussion of the cards and metaphors in their own cultures. Participants should feel free to apply their own interpretations to the cards or even to make up their own metaphors by writing or drawing on a separate piece of paper.

Because the cards are labeled in English, managers may find it more challenging to use Leadership Metaphor Explorer with non- or limited-English speakers. One solution is to ask those participants to ignore the labels and simply respond to the drawings.

How Does Leadership Metaphor Explorer Work?

Leadership Metaphor Explorer is beginner-friendly, and it's usually not necessary to understand all of the theory and research behind it. In fact, the facilitator often needs to stay out of the way and let people engage with the tool and with each other. Leadership Metaphor Explorer works by putting something tangible—the cards—into the middle of what might otherwise be an abstract conversation (Palus & Drath, 2001). Simply asking people to talk using the cards as visual props helps the dynamics of the conversation. Using the cards reduces stress and increases engagement. The tone of these mediated conversations tends to be insightful and

A CORE OF SELF-AWARENESS

Sarah Miller, a CCL colleague, used Leadership Metaphor Explorer in a conversation with Buddhist monks in Thailand.

The first time we talked, M. told us that monks are supposed to be leaders in the community and that he, particularly, was interested in social justice. During our second conversation, we brought out the Leadership Metaphor Explorer cards. M. chose two cards: one to answer the question of how a monk should be a leader in the community and one to answer the question of how he wished to be a leader. The two intersected at the theme of "know thyself." For M., the most important part of leadership is knowing oneself because only then can one lead others. M. also chose other cards to represent the various aspects of leadership that a monk exhibits. But at the heart of his understanding lay self-awareness.

Figure 2. A young monk in a monastery contemplates Leadership Metaphor Explorer's metaphors and their relation to self-awareness.

respectful rather than confrontational. Everyone gets to share his or her cards and comment on the other cards, leveling the power relations and relaxing the participants.

Humans depend heavily on their sense of sight. Humans are also highly communicative. Sometimes, when faced with a challenge, people will try to talk themselves through it. Leadership Metaphor Explorer opens up a different channel, granting insight and information that flows through visual, emotional, physical, and nonverbal channels.

Metaphor—the act of comparing the qualities of two different things as if they were the same—is at the root of human cognition and self-identity (Mair, 1977; McAdams, 1997), and perhaps of consciousness itself (Dennett, 1991; Jaynes, 1976). We know that metaphors can be a powerful aid to thinking and communicating when used with intention and discipline (Lakoff & Johnson, 2003). When Leadership Metaphor Explorer injects metaphors into strategic conversations, new insights and ideas emerge.

Part of the problem in thinking about leadership is that the topic is full of clichés and platitudes. Ideas about leadership run in predictable ruts. We miss opportunities to practice leadership because we have trouble thinking about options and alternatives. For example, people will focus on "the leader as hero" and miss the options inherent in "the leader as servant" or "the leader as coach." Leadership Metaphor Explorer offers people new metaphors that can direct them to new opportunities.

Do we want people to model themselves literally as Dependable Repairmen (to quote one card)? No. We want them to explore metaphorical connotations such as dependable, loyal, service oriented, and problem solving as potentially helpful for their own situations.

How Does Leadership Metaphor Explorer Address Leadership Types?

Leadership Metaphor Explorer's design accommodates three distinct types of leadership metaphors. In the first type, leadership is associated with authority, power, dominance, and control. CCL calls this dependent leadership. Leadership based in influence, expertise, heroic effort, and individual ambition comes next. CCL refers to this as independent leadership. Finally, there is a type of leadership based in collaboration, diverse perspectives, shared learning, and intentional boundary spanning. This is interdependent leadership (Drath, Palus, & McGuire, 2010). Each of Leadership Metaphor Explorer's cards is coded according to these three types, with red labels for dependent, green labels for independent, and blue labels for interdependent. Because Leadership Metaphor Explorer is based on metaphor, the coding is open to interpretation, and many of the metaphors may fit more than one type.

	Dependent Culture of Conformity	**Independent** Culture of Cooperation and/or Consensus	**Interdependent** Culture of Collaboration
Direction comes from . . .	People at the top having clear authority	All parties having authority (often relies upon designated representatives)	The people who lead collaboration having authority based on larger strategic intent
Alignment comes from . . .	Conforming to established rules and procedures	Cooperation and negotiation across functional silos and geographies	Real-time collaboration and sense making across multiple stakeholders
Commitment comes from . . .	Loyalty	Enlightened self-interest	Engagement in a larger purpose than self
Ideal organizational structure . . .	Hierarchy	Matrix or small group	Cross-organizational network
Works best in . . .	Stable and defined environment, or times of crisis	Highly segmented businesses or certain functions (e.g., sales)	Growth and innovation companies, or when cross-company work is critical

Figure 3. Characteristics of leadership types.

Dependent leadership cultures are characterized by the belief that only people in positions of authority are responsible for leadership. This assumption may lead to organizations that emphasize top-down control and deference to authority. In general, dependent cultures can be thought of as conformer cultures.

Dependent leadership cultures and independent leadership cultures have limits to their capability to produce direction, alignment, and commitment. When the clients or customers demand fully integrated service across lines of business, the value of heroic, independent leadership can fall short of meeting that demand.

Independent leadership cultures are characterized by the belief that leadership emerges from individuals based on their knowledge and expertise. This assumption may lead to decentralized decision making, high demand for individual responsibility, and competition among types of experts. In general, independent cultures can be thought of as achiever cultures.

Interdependent leadership cultures are characterized by the belief that leadership is a collective activity that requires mutual inquiry and learning (McCauley et al., 2008). This assumption may lead to the widespread use of dialogue, collaboration, horizontal networks, the valuing of differences, and a focus on learning. In general, interdependent cultures can be thought of as collaborative cultures. As they develop from dependent to independent to interdependent, leadership cultures gain capacity to deal with complexity and ambiguity.

Interdependence isn't an ideal. Only a small fraction of organizations meet the criteria of interdependence (Kegan, 1994; McCauley et al., 2008; Torbert, 2004). There are highly successful dependent and independent organizations in business, in communities, in governments, and in NGOs. Organizations may exhibit all three leadership types. For example, an organization that provides mental health services might exhibit a dependent culture in its support staff, an independent culture among its case workers, and an interdependent culture in its relations among these parts and with external stakeholders.

Levels of leadership. CCL defines leadership in terms of outcomes—direction, alignment, and commitment. Those outcomes can be observed at different levels of leadership action: society, organization, group, and individual.

The societal level includes relationships among organizations, across entire fields and industries, and among regional cultures (Ospina & Foldy, 2010; Quinn & Van Velsor, 2010). The organizational level includes multipart organizations and communities. The group level includes smaller organizational collectives such as divisions, functions, teams, work groups, and task forces. The individual level includes the qualities and subjective viewpoints of individual leaders, followers, and members.

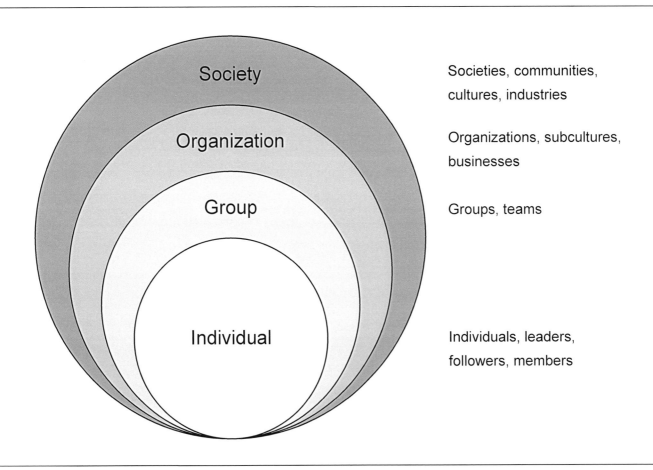

Figure 4. Four levels of leadership.

Each leadership level provides leverage for development. All four levels can be identified as vital in any scenario in which direction, alignment, and commitment are produced. Our research and experience suggest that attention to processes and outcomes at all four levels are necessary for developing more collaborative, interdependent leadership.

When Should Leadership Metaphor Explorer Be Used?

Leadership Metaphor Explorer should be used with individuals or groups when they need fresh insight about their leadership and its development. Typically, that need arises in the face of complex challenges, or what Bob Johansen (2012) calls VUCA: conditions of increasing volatility, uncertainty, complexity, and ambiguity. Those conditions pervade contemporary life. Leadership Metaphor Explorer offers a means to achieve direction, alignment, and commitment in response to the VUCA world, no matter where you are. You can use Leadership Metaphor Explorer on the bus, at the dinner table, in a class, or in a team meeting. It's portable enough for impromptu meetings. It supports great conversations in a serious and formal atmosphere, and it supports great conversations when humor and levity are welcome.

Leadership Metaphor Explorer is a wonderful tool that lends itself to a wide range of leadership, cultural, and community-building explorations at an individual or group level, and those explorations are a valuable reflection and discussion tool for leadership coaches.

—*Jim Myracle, cofounder and partner, TMT Associates, Inc.*

Why Should Leadership Metaphor Explorer Be Used?

Leadership Metaphor Explorer helps you see your present leadership approach more clearly, and it helps you imagine the leadership approach needed in the future. Related benefits include the following:

- Creates shared understanding about the challenges at hand
- Creates fresh, memorable metaphors and stories about a complex challenge that engage people in finding solutions

- Builds safety for self-disclosure and vulnerability
- Improves interpersonal understanding and trust
- Promotes self-reflection
- Elicits new questions and alternatives
- Helps people envision a better future
- Helps people see their environment and their organization with fresh eyes
- Legitimizes intuition and emotion
- Generates alternative futures for wiser planning
- Encourages fun, playful, yet serious dialogue
- Taps into personal experiences and passions
- Makes abstract conversations tangible
- Frames and illustrates thoughts so they can be shared
- Surfaces individual and group assumptions
- Spans boundaries, contexts, and cultures
- Helps people move from ineffective positions
- Produces tangible images that can be reused in paper and digital forms

Who Can Conduct a Leadership Metaphor Explorer Session?

Most people can facilitate a basic Leadership Metaphor Explorer session. In most cases, it's sufficient to follow the instructions in this guide and to provide some basic directions to the participants. The facilitator's job is simple and unobtrusive: to support a good conversation among the group members. That job usually requires only a beginner's level of facilitation skill. Beyond this, the facilitator needs only the skills that match the goals of any specific Leadership Metaphor Explorer session. For example, to conduct strategic planning, the group needs a facilitator with some experience in strategic planning. For sessions that may surface conflict, a facilitator should be able to handle tough, emotional situations. Experienced hands at organizational change are needed when Leadership Metaphor Explorer is used in a long-term transformation initiative.

Preparing for a Leadership Metaphor Explorer Session

The following questions will help you prepare for your Leadership Metaphor Explorer session:

- What outcomes do you hope to achieve?
- Do you have a colleague who can check the design and offer honest input and feedback?
- Can you do a practice session first?
- Who will participate in the session? Will you have the right people in the room?
- Why are you using Leadership Metaphor Explorer? How will you describe the benefits for this particular group?
- Do you have at least 30 minutes for the session? Do you have enough time to get the outcomes you want?
- Do you have the Leadership Metaphor Explorer deck at your disposal? One deck is typically enough for about five people. The more framing questions you ask, the more cards you need—one card (at least) per person per question.
- How will the participants browse the cards? Will they use their own tabletops, or will a separate browsing area be provided? Will each person get a deck?
- What are your framing questions? How might you improve them? (Read the suggestions for creating good framing questions on page 22.)
- Will you assign a note taker to capture the conversation? Can you use groupware or presentation software to project the discussion in real time on a shared display?
- What guidelines will you use regarding confidentiality?
- How will you capture and compose the results of the session? For example, will you use a camera to record the cards selected?
- If your Leadership Metaphor Explorer session is part of a larger organizational initiative, does the overall agenda include a plan to continue the dialogue and create next steps?

- Will the group use the metaphors it selects and its discussion notes to communicate the results of the session to stakeholders inside and outside the organization?
- How will you follow up on the insights gained from the session? Are you ready to create an action plan?

Creating Effective Framing Questions

Effective framing questions are the key to a successful Leadership Metaphor Explorer session. An effective framing question is one that elicits the right conversation. The right conversation (in most situations) is one that is open, insightful, and honest; it gets down to the essence of the challenge or topic at hand. The wrong conversation is one in which people converse about a topic they don't find important or in which people remain closed to each other.

Determine what the group wants or needs to explore. Compose a few alternative ways to ask the framing questions, and then try them out with one or more of the participants before the session. You may be surprised at how a question can be interpreted differently from what you had in mind.

You can frame questions about leadership at societal, organizational, group, or individual levels. Try framing your leadership question at more than just one of the levels. For more complex challenges and comprehensive leadership strategies, you need to go up to the levels of organizational culture and societal beliefs and practices for creating direction, alignment, and commitment.

Here are some sample framing questions and statements, divided among the different levels of leadership. Using the pattern below, you can fashion questions that double as instructions for choosing cards:

Choose a card that says something about (or represents) . . .

The right number of framing questions is often two: one for now and one for the future.

Individual Level

What kind of leader am I? What kind of leader do I want to be?

Which behaviors do I do too much? Not enough? Just right?

What qualities do I need to develop?

What are my strengths as a leader? My weaknesses?

This is me at my best . . . at my worst . . . under stress.

This is me with subordinates . . . with peers . . . with bosses . . . with customers.

How do others see me?

This is me when I was younger . . . now . . . next year.

This is what an effective leader does. This is what an ineffective leader does.

Group or Team Level

How do we relate to each other on this team? How do we relate to other teams or functions in the organization?

What kind of leadership does this team need? What kind do we have now?

How do we practice leadership across the boundaries that separate us from other teams?

Think of the best team you have been a part of. How did that team practice leadership?

Think of the worst team you have been a part of. How did that team practice leadership?

How do we create direction, alignment, and commitment?

This is us at our best. This is us at our worst.

This is what we looked like during the last crisis we faced.

This is what we look like to other groups or teams . . . to our sponsor.

Organizational or Cultural Level

What does leadership look like here? What kind of culture do we have? What kind of leadership culture do we need?

Given the future we want to achieve, describe the people that will create and inhabit this future.

What kind of leadership do we need for the challenges we face?

How do we create direction, alignment, and commitment that is unique to our culture?

What would it look like if we had a culture of innovation?

How do our subcultures or functions practice leadership?

How do we practice leadership across boundaries, with other teams, with other organizations?

This is how we can transform the leadership culture in our organization (past, present, and future).

What does our leadership strategy need to look like?

This is the kind of talent we have in this organization.

This is the kind of talent we want to develop or bring into this organization.

Societal or Community Level

What does our competitors' leadership culture look like?

How should we relate to each of our clients or customers?

How can we be successful in our market?

How can we transform leadership in our market?

This is typical behavior in our industry. This is how our industry needs to improve. This is how we can be leaders in our market, field, or industry.

How do we relate to people who are like us? How do we relate to people who are not like us?

What was leadership like in my community where I grew up? How did my parents practice leadership in the family . . . in the community?

What is the legacy we want to leave to our community?

What does our community need from us?

What kind of world do we want to live in? What kind of world do we want for our grandchildren?

Conducting a Leadership Metaphor Explorer Session

Leadership Metaphor Explorer is a tool rather than a scripted exercise—many useful alternatives and options are possible. We recommend practicing first with yourself and one other person. A minimum of 30 minutes is typically required for a basic Leadership Metaphor Explorer session with a small group. An impromptu and quick session can be done one-on-one in less time. Leadership Metaphor Explorer sessions typically lead into further conversations and developmental planning, team building, visioning, and so on. There are five steps in conducting a Leadership Metaphor Explorer session: prepare, frame, browse, reflect and converse, and extend.

Step-by-Step Instructions

Prepare. Think about the purpose of the session. Get the right people in the room. Refer to the list of framing questions on pages 23–24. Make sure you have enough cards.

Frame. Introduce the session to the group in a way that's appropriate to the group's norms. Discuss the goals of the session and what might happen as a result. Discuss confidentiality as appropriate. Listen to questions the group members ask, and respond.

Leadership Metaphor Explorer typically works well without formally introducing the underlying theories of leadership, metaphors, and so on. Save that for after the session, as needed—that's when people will be most engaged and excited. Leadership Metaphor Explorer is effective at engaging people and drawing them out. Too much talking by the facilitator can hamper the process. Simply invite the group into a conversation about leadership and then use Leadership Metaphor Explorer to get out of usual habits and try something fresh.

Share the session schedule with the group. Summarize the steps. Give them the framing questions or statements couched in language that is natural for the group. You can phrase the questions in different ways for particular groups. Post the questions where everyone can refer to them throughout the session.

Browse. Spread out one or more Leadership Metaphor Explorer decks for everyone to look at. You can use a tabletop, other furniture, or the floor. Some people like to line the cards up in straight rows; others like to spread them in a loose pile. Or you can give a deck to each person to thumb through.

Depending on the number of people and framing questions, you may need several decks. As a rule of thumb, one Leadership Metaphor Explorer deck is enough for about five people sharing a tabletop for browsing.

Figure 5. A group browses Leadership Metaphor Explorer cards at the MiL Institute, Klippan, Sweden.

If you have a large number of people in the session, more than 30 or so, you may need to use a creative way of browsing. For example, give each person three random cards in an envelope and then instruct the participants to find their choices among all the cards in the room.

Ask people to choose a card that answers or represents each framing question or statement. You might say

- Choose a card for each question (see flip chart or slide for the questions).
- Pick a card that you can relate to, that speaks to you.
- Don't overthink this. Use your intuition.
- Sometimes the card picks you!
- You can pick a card even if you don't know what it means. You can decide what it means.
- You can even create your own metaphor.

Figure 6. Bank workers browse Leadership Metaphor Explorer cards in Mumbai, India.

You have options regarding how many cards each person chooses in response to each question. Choosing one card generally helps focus the conversation quickly. Often people can't help themselves and choose several cards for each question. Unless you don't have enough cards, don't worry about people choosing more than one.

Another option is for people to choose all of the cards that they think apply to each question. The ensuing conversation can involve sorting through the many choices and reflecting on themes and patterns. After the group has identified themes, you can ask participants to choose the best card for each theme. Choosing a lot of cards for each question often leads to a session that is fun, fast, and semichaotic, as people scramble to make sense of all the choices and arrange them into some kind of order.

For a change of pace, ask people to pick from facedown cards so that they can't see the metaphor. Or simply give them a random card. Then ask them to relate the card to the question in some way or give them a list of possible questions to which they can relate the card.

Reflect and converse. Ask each group to discuss the cards they selected. Consider using some of the following questions to help participants get started. Reflection questions relate to the session's framing questions. Post some reflection questions where everyone can see them.

- Why did you choose each card? What does it mean to you?
- How are your cards and your reasons for choosing them similar to or different from mine?
- How do you interpret the cards that I picked? What does each of my cards mean to you?
- What patterns do we see among the cards we chose? How do we interpret those patterns?
- What do I or we need to stop doing? Start doing? Continue doing?

During this part of the session, the facilitator should allow conversations among participants to flow freely. Note any concerns about the process, the choices, the interpretations—anything that brings conversation to a halt. Encourage the group to keep going even if it feels stuck. Improvise as needed.

Figure 7. Sharing Leadership Metaphor Explorer cards. What do you see? What does it mean to you?

Often the same cards come up when session participants work in the same organization, especially if each person has his or her own deck. Note similarities and return to them; consolidate these key metaphors and their interpretations.

Exploring differences in card selection within a single organization can also provoke an insightful conversation. Do the themes suggest that different subcultures (dependent, independent, interdependent) operate in the organization? How does each create direction, alignment, and commitment for itself, and what effect does that have on direction, alignment, and commitment throughout the organization?

Extend. A Leadership Metaphor Explorer session can continue, and its conversation can grow deeper over time, especially if the dialogue is tied to leadership development at all levels (society, organization, group, individual). Groups that participate in separate sessions can begin to accumulate insights that bridge gaps between them. Further, the organization can plan leadership development initiatives to meet the future desired state, thus putting into place a leadership strategy. Preserve the cards (or copies—print and electronic), along with descriptive text, photos, and action plans, for use in reports and for furthering the discussion formally or through asynchronous methods, such as discussion groups on the organization's intranet.

Options

Apply these Leadership Metaphor Explorer options and alternatives alone or in combination:

- Conduct an initial discussion of the current shared challenge. For example, you can frame such a discussion as a response to new

Figure 8. A small group charts current and future states of leadership.

information, such as the CEO's recent company address or an outside expert's report on market dynamics.

- Bring together groups with shared work across five kinds of boundaries (horizontal, vertical, stakeholder, demographic, and geographic). First, have the conversation within groups. Then compare notes (a "gallery walk" of each other's charts) and continue the conversations, this time among people across the boundaries.

- Discuss how each metaphor or theme indicates or speaks against direction, alignment, and commitment as outcomes of leadership.

- Introduce the idea of leadership culture as how the organization as a whole views and practices leadership and creates direction, alignment, and commitment. Explore leadership subcultures within and across different groups in the organization.

- Ask the group or groups to come to a consensus on just one card to represent the present state of leadership (at one or more levels) and one other card for the imagined future state of leadership.

- Photograph the group responses that you've written on flip charts and share them online (in accordance with confidentiality agreements).

- Ask people about the cards they did *not* choose—why not?

- Ask each person to select one or more cards that describe his or her own leadership style, beliefs, and behaviors. Later, these cards can be used in one-on-one coaching conversations and for self-reflection—for example, What approach to leadership might I use to be more effective?

- Give people time to reflect and write in journals at various points during the session.

- Explore the definitions of *leadership* that come up in the conversation. For example, some participants may have chosen cards that suggest leadership is based on occupying the top positions in the organization. Others may have selected cards that illustrate ideas of leadership as operating throughout the organization.

Designer's Tip

Practice using Leadership Metaphor Explorer in a small setting before using it with larger groups. That way, you can get comfortable in setting it up, developing the framing questions, and so on. For example, use it one-on-one with a colleague or friend to explore something like the leadership you have experienced when you are at your most creative and the leadership you have experienced when your creativity is stifled. Get used to hearing the stories that emerge and engaging in the conversations that ensue.

- If you're prepared to discuss the different types of leadership, you can reveal the card caption colors, which are red for dependent leadership, green for independent, and blue for interdependent. Be aware, however, that the type represented also depends on the subjective meaning making of the participant.
- Discuss the four levels of leadership beliefs, behaviors, and practices (society, organization, group, individual) and their connection to present and future challenges. Is leadership an individual role, a collective activity, or both?

Leadership Metaphor Explorer Applications

In this section, we introduce a variety of uses for Leadership Metaphor Explorer that facilitators can apply in different situations and for moving toward specific outcomes. The applications cover all levels of leadership development: individual, group or team, organization or community, and society.

Individual
    Self-Coaching
    One-on-One Coaching

Group or Team
    Team Coaching
    Business School Classroom

Organization or Community
    Leadership Strategy
    Innovation Leadership
    Leadership Culture
    Talent Management

Society
    Boundary Spanning
    Scenario Creation

APPLICATION: SELF-COACHING

Personal reflection is important in gaining insight and clarity about your own development as a leader and follower. Leadership Metaphor Explorer can support these inner conversations by combining images and metaphors that focus your thoughts.

Facilitation

Simple questions can lead to deep insights: What kind of leader am I now? What kind of leader do I want to be in the future? What are my strengths? What do I need to develop to be that future leader?

The individual can ask questions related to any level of leadership, including reflection on his or her group, organization, and society: What does leadership look like in my team? My organization? How can I begin to positively change the communities in which I live?

Keep the Leadership Metaphor Explorer deck handy for moments of impromptu self-reflection or to elicit coaching from others. Invite others to choose a card that represents how they see you at your best and another that represents how they see you at your worst.

Benefits of This Application

- Empowers self-coaching
- Taps into personal experiences and passions
- Surfaces individual and group assumptions
- Creates new metaphors
- Elicits new questions and alternatives
- Generates alternative futures for wiser planning
- Legitimizes intuition and emotion
- Helps people move from ineffective positions
- Produces tangible images that can be reused in paper and digital forms

Additional Resources for This Application

King & Altman. *Discovering the leader in you workbook.*

King, Altman, & Lee. *Discovering the leader in you.*

Van Velsor, McCauley, & Ruderman. *The Center for Creative Leadership handbook of leadership development.*

Example of This Application in Action

Our colleague Dave Lewis keeps a Leadership Metaphor Explorer deck on top of his desk where visitors see it. He looks at it occasionally when he is thinking about his projects and needs a fresh idea. "I'll take a break from the computer screen and flip through them. It helps me think about why other people act the way they do and why I respond the way I do. The drawings are interesting, and it's kind of relaxing to just browse through them."

Visitors are often curious about the deck on Dave's desk and pick it up." Leadership Metaphor Explorer is a social lubricant. It's good for a laugh, and sometimes they really get into it and talk about work, their frustrations, or their coworkers. They talk about particular people or a situation they're in."

APPLICATION: ONE-ON-ONE COACHING

CCL's approach to one-on-one coaching uses a framework called RACSR, for *relationship, assessment, challenge, support,* and *results.* This framework calls for establishing, building, and maintaining a relationship with the coachee; using assessments to help the coachee make sense of his or her challenges as well as strengths and development needs; challenging the coachee to develop; supporting the coachee throughout the coaching engagement; and helping the coachee get such results as committing to developmental actions and being accountable. Leadership Metaphor Explorer supports the assessment, challenge, and results part of the coaching framework.

Facilitation

The facilitation for this application is much like that done in group work and other individual leader development work. The facilitator offers the coachee a deck of Leadership Metaphor Explorer cards and asks him or her to select a card that generally describes how he or she presently sees himself or herself. The coach asks follow-up questions: Where would you like to be in order to resolve the challenge you are facing? How might you develop in addressing the challenge?

Example of This Application in Action

In this example, the coachee was the CEO of a company in the construction industry. The CEO had set a challenge for the organization to

Benefits of This Application

- Improves interpersonal understanding and trust
- Promotes self-reflection
- Elicits new questions and alternatives
- Generates alternative futures for wiser planning
- Taps into personal experiences and passions
- Surfaces individual and group assumptions
- Helps people move from ineffective positions

become more innovative. After three years of emphasizing this in the organization and even declaring a substantial budget for innovative projects, there had been no movement; no one had stepped up to offer a project that might possibly lead to an innovation for the company and potentially for the industry. The CEO talked with his coach about the culture of the company—in particular, the leadership culture. The coach offered the CEO a Leadership Metaphor Explorer deck and asked him to sort through the cards and select two: one for the leadership as it appeared to him currently and a second one that characterized the leadership culture needed to sustain the company as an innovative company.

The CEO went further. He selected a card to represent the culture in place immediately before he took the reins, several cards for the current state of the company's leadership culture, another card representing a move toward an innovative organization, and two more cards: one for where he believed the organization could get to during his tenure and one for an ideal culture that he didn't believe could be achieved during his tenure but for which the organization should strive. The ensuing coaching exchange explored the stories behind each of the CEO's selections (see Figure 9, page 38, for a portion of the storyboard). After this session, the CEO shared the storyboard and initiated a dialogue with his executive team and, in particular, with the senior VP of human resources.

All of this process can be classified as challenge, in that it provided a different way for the coachee to make sense of and explore his challenge.

Additional Resources for This Application

McAdams. *The stories we live by.*
Palus & Drath. Putting something in the middle.
Palus & Horth. *The leader's edge.*
Sewerin. *Leadership, teams and coaching.*
Ting & Riddle. A framework for leadership development coaching.
Whyte. *Crossing the unknown sea.*
Wilber. *Integral psychology.*

Assessment comprises the selection of the cards covering where the company came from and how the leadership culture is currently. Results are seen in both possible and ideal futures.

The company was formed by bringing multiple companies together.

Like player-coaches, we are not giving ourselves time to stand back and reflect—to think strategically.

We got to where we are today through our operational efficiency— a legacy from the previous CEO's focus on 6 Sigma.

Figure 9. A portion of the CEO's storyboard.

APPLICATION: TEAM COACHING

Effective team coaching combines action and reflection (O'Neil & Marsick, 2007; Rimanoczy & Turner, 2008). But it can be hard to reflect as a team. One approach is to use powerful questions to drive an open dialogue. Leadership Metaphor Explorer is an effective tool for framing and exploring these questions, as it allows groups to "put something in the middle" and so defuse an otherwise difficult conversation.

Facilitation

Because the basic instructions for Leadership Metaphor Explorer are oriented to small-group situations and team coaching, facilitation follows those guidelines.

Example of This Application in Action

Here's a field report from Tom Hickok. Tom is an adjunct professor in the School of Public Administration and Policy at Virginia Tech, as

Benefits of This Application

- Creates shared understanding about the challenges at hand
- Creates fresh, memorable metaphors and stories about a complex challenge that engage people in finding solutions
- Builds safety for self-disclosure and vulnerability
- Improves interpersonal understanding and trust
- Elicits new questions and alternatives
- Helps people envision a better future
- Helps people see their environment and their organization with fresh eyes
- Generates alternative futures for wiser planning
- Encourages fun, playful, yet serious dialogue
- Taps into personal experiences and passions
- Produces tangible images that can be reused in paper and digital forms
- Helps people move from ineffective positions

well as a consultant to the U.S. Department of Defense in the areas of IT strategic planning, program oversight, and workforce development.

> I used the Leadership Metaphor Explorer cards yesterday in a team-building off-site. The group that I support in the Department of Defense environment almost doubled in the last few months, from about 18 to about 30. The off-site was planned to be largely a fun event for this group, with pizza lunch and time afterward to socialize and relax. But there was a team-building exercise at the front end, and I used the Leadership Metaphor Explorer cards as part of it.
>
> The design of the exercise was for the division director to make some comments about some changes ahead. The purpose of those comments was to get the group thinking seriously about change management. When the director finished speaking, I followed on his talk with the theme of initiating change within a sea of change. After a word about the purpose of team building, I asked the 23 participants to browse the cards and pick one that they related to in some way, or that spoke to them about the challenges or opportunities ahead. They did that and reconvened, with chairs arranged in a circle to allow good face-to-face contact.
>
> I asked them to share briefly about why they picked the card they did, and any brief story behind it. Everybody shared willingly, without extra pressure. A few people shared about parts of their personal background that were previously undisclosed.

Additional Resources for This Application

Frankovelgia & Martineau. Coaching teams.
O'Neil & Marsick. *Understanding action learning.*
Palus & Horth. *The leader's edge.*
Rimanoczy & Turner. *Action reflection learning.*
Sewerin. *Leadership, teams and coaching.*

Others talked about their work goals. Comments afterward were very positive about the experience.

Some things to note: The Leadership Metaphor Explorer exercise was compressed to about 35 minutes because we started as lunch approached, and I didn't want to start a hunger strike. My design consideration in having the whole group share instead of breaking into subgroups was to help facilitate relationships across the whole team. Also, the limited time didn't really support a two-step feedback process (small teams to large teams). I kept the sharing very short because of the time constraints. We could have productively shared much longer (at least another hour), I believe. "

Business school classrooms suffering from a lack of student engagement can enliven the discussion with Leadership Metaphor Explorer. A Leadership Metaphor Explorer session can be fun and at the same time enable serious conversations. Instructors can use Leadership Metaphor Explorer to frame and teach concepts of leadership and to question students about their own perspectives and experiences of leadership.

Facilitation

The basic instructions for Leadership Metaphor Explorer apply to this application. The instructor's overall curriculum design can be infused with content about leadership and culture for a more comprehensive learning experience.

Benefits of This Application

- Builds safety for self-disclosure and vulnerability
- Promotes self-reflection
- Improves interpersonal understanding and trust
- Elicits new questions and alternatives
- Helps people see their environment and their organization with fresh eyes
- Legitimizes intuition and emotion
- Encourages fun, playful, yet serious dialogue
- Taps into personal experiences and passions
- Makes abstract conversations tangible
- Surfaces individual and group assumptions
- Spans boundaries, contexts, and cultures
- Creates fresh, memorable metaphors and stories about a complex challenge that engage people in finding solutions
- Produces tangible images that can be reused in paper and digital forms
- Helps people move from ineffective positions

Example of This Application in Action

Charles J. (Chuck) Palus and his daughter Shannon used Leadership Metaphor Explorer at the Harvard Business School at a symposium titled How Can Leadership Be Taught. The symposium was aimed at creating a shared body of knowledge about teaching leadership. Presenters tried to convey what the experience (not just content) of teaching and learning leadership is like. One overarching theme of the symposium was the distinction between developing individual leaders and developing collective leadership processes. Teachers often focus on the individual leader because their classes are filled with individual students. But there are times when teachers work with the cultural and organizational beliefs and practices operating in the classroom as a social system.

As an example of the latter, Chuck discussed leadership culture and its logics of dependence, independence, and interdependence. A challenge to teaching and implementing these ideas is that, while individual leaders and their behaviors are singular and visible, leadership culture can be difficult to grasp. In such cases, development includes practicing the kinds of attention that make culture and distributed forms of leadership more visible and tangible, thus allowing teachers and students to view culture more objectively.

Chuck describes how he used Leadership Metaphor Explorer:

" I asked the group to reflect on the following questions and to write responses in their journals or on a piece of paper: How is leadership done where you work? What does it typically look like in action? What is the leadership culture of your workplace?

Next, I gave the group these instructions: "Taped under your desk you will find an envelope with three cards. Trade and exchange cards with anyone in the room. Find one card that especially fits or illustrates your response to one or more of the questions." (Half of the envelopes had Visual Explorer cards—another CCL dialogue tool, which has cards with images only—and half had Leadership Metaphor Explorer cards.)

I continued with these instructions: "Now find a partner or two near you. Share your cards in two ways. First, what are the

McGuire, Palus, Pasmore, & Rhodes. *Transforming your organization.*

Palus. How can leadership be taught.

Palus, McGuire, & Ernst. Developing interdependent leadership.

Palus, McGuire, & Rhodes. Evolving your leadership culture.

details of the card itself? Next, what does the card mean to you, and why did you pick it? After sharing your cards, take another minute and jot down key insights from the conversation you just had."

The ensuing conversations were vibrant and serious, with lots of laughter. People connected very positively and helped each other develop insights about the topic and their relationship to it. The cards and creative conversations helped make culture more visible.

APPLICATION: LEADERSHIP STRATEGY

Often the leadership strategy of an organization is vague or taken for granted (Pasmore & Lafferty, 2009). Leadership Metaphor Explorer helps make the leadership strategy more explicit and intentionally connected to the business strategy, by helping people understand the different functions of dependent, independent, and interdependent leadership (Palus, McGuire, & Ernst, 2011). Leadership Metaphor Explorer gets at key leadership strategy questions: What kinds of leadership will we need in the future, given our business strategy (and mission and vision)? What kinds of leadership do we have now? How must we work differently with each other so that we can be successful?

Facilitation

The basic instructions for Leadership Metaphor Explorer apply. The facilitator needs to have experience and skill commensurate with the group and situation. Sustained strategy work requires more than Leadership Metaphor Explorer sessions.

Benefits of This Application

- Creates shared understanding about the challenges at hand
- Builds safety for self-disclosure and vulnerability
- Elicits new questions and alternatives
- Helps people envision a better future
- Helps people see their environment and their organization with fresh eyes
- Legitimizes intuition and emotion
- Generates alternative futures for wiser planning
- Encourages fun, playful, yet serious dialogue
- Taps into personal experiences and passions

I often describe the use of these cards and their companion, Visual Explorer, as greasing the wheels of conversation.

—*Bruce Flye*

Example of This Application in Action

Bruce Flye used Leadership Metaphor Explorer for a week-long planning institute for the National Association of College and University Food Service. He used an approach to planning and strategy called Idealized Design (Ackoff, Magidson, & Addison, 2006). Bruce describes how he used Leadership Metaphor Explorer:

> Idealized Design begins with a systems analysis of the current situation, in this instance provided by a fictionalized case study representing a campus with an assortment of similar issues. Once the participants' analyses were complete, we asked them to consider the current leadership culture. To do this, we used Leadership Metaphor Explorer, a tool developed by the Center for Creative Leadership with a little help from yours truly. All of the cards were spread out on a table, and we asked the 18 participants to review each. They then picked the one that seemed most like their situation or, if none seemed to work, they picked the card that spoke to them in some way.
>
> As they were working in three groups of six, we asked them to return to their groups and then share their cards and their thinking in turn. Each group was then asked to agree on two cards from their six that seemed to best represent the leadership culture in place on this fictional campus. We then took the two cards from each group and set them aside without discussion.
>
> As the week went by, they developed their Idealized Designs. Pretty quickly, they produced this mission statement:
>
>> Walnut College Food Service exists to provide students with healthy and sustainable food options in an environment that enables them to become successful individuals.

Once each group had drafted its Idealized Design, we borrowed from Appreciative Inquiry and crafted Provocative Propositions to guide the subsequent work as opposed to the traditional gap analysis.

Once they had worked their way through the additional details, we asked them to return to a question of leadership: What is the leadership culture that will give life to the Idealized Design and its Provocative Propositions? We repeated the selection of metaphor cards, and then posted both sets for comparison.

The original six, as they described them, depicted a conservative and insular environment. Confluence of Agendas to them represented people each getting something for themselves while the larger whole slowly deteriorated. Leaderless Orchestra to them was an indication of a poorly functioning entity. With the new set, they were quick to see a distinct shift toward an interdependent leadership culture. Even metaphors not normally associated with interdependency had a role in creating it: Nurturing Parents reflected the fact that someone would have to teach these new skills and behaviors; High-Performance Engines described how the college's senior leadership was going to have to step up its game in order to keep up with the dining services group.

Additional Resources for This Application

Ackoff, Magidson, & Addison. *Idealized design.*

Beatty & Byington. Developing strategic leadership.

Hughes & Beatty. *Becoming a strategic leader.*

Hughes, Ginnett, & Curphy. *Leadership.*

Hughes, Palus, Ernst, Houston, & McGuire. Boundary spanning across leadership cultures.

Palus, Horth, Pulley, & Selvin. Exploration for development.

Palus, McGuire, & Ernst. Developing interdependent leadership.

Pasmore & Lafferty. *Developing a leadership strategy.*

van der Heijden. *Scenarios.*

APPLICATION: INNOVATION LEADERSHIP

To make sense of unfamiliar situations and complex challenges, we must have a grasp of the whole of the situation, including its variables, unknowns, and mysterious forces. This requires skills beyond everyday analysis. It requires innovation leadership. Innovation leadership has two components (Horth & Buchner, 2009):

1. An approach to leadership that brings new thinking and different actions to how you lead, manage, and go about your work.

    - How can you think differently about your role and the challenges you and your organization face?

Benefits of This Application

- Creates shared understanding about the challenges at hand
- Creates fresh, memorable metaphors and stories about a complex challenge that engage people in finding solutions
- Builds safety for self-disclosure and vulnerability
- Improves interpersonal understanding and trust
- Elicits new questions and alternatives
- Helps people envision a better future
- Helps people see their environment and their organization with fresh eyes
- Legitimizes intuition and emotion
- Generates alternative futures for wiser planning
- Encourages fun, playful, yet serious dialogue
- Taps into personal experiences and passions
- Makes abstract conversations tangible
- Frames and illustrates thoughts so they can be shared
- Surfaces individual and group assumptions
- Spans boundaries, contexts, and cultures
- Produces tangible images that can be reused in paper and digital forms
- Helps people move from ineffective positions

- What can you do to break open entrenched, intractable problems? How can you be agile and quick in the absence of information or predictability?

2. Leadership for innovation that allows leaders to learn how to create an organizational climate where others apply innovative thinking to solve problems and develop new products and services. Such leadership grows a culture of innovation—it doesn't merely hire a few creative outliers.

    - How can you help others to think differently and work in new ways to face challenges?
    - What can be done to innovate when all resources are stressed and constrained?
    - How can you stay alive and stay ahead of the competition?

Leadership Metaphor Explorer is a modest yet effective tool to support either or both of these ideas, fostering an innovative approach to leadership, as well as leadership for innovation.

Facilitation

The basic instructions for Leadership Metaphor Explorer apply. The facilitator needs to have experience and skill commensurate with the group and situation. Participants should first be introduced to the topic of innovation in a manner relevant to their situation. Sustained innovation requires more than Leadership Metaphor Explorer sessions.

Example of This Application in Action

Jim Myracle, cofounder and partner, TMT Associates, Inc., used Leadership Metaphor Explorer cards to support a learning module on leading innovation. The objective was to understand the leadership behaviors and cultural attributes enabling innovation. Since this module was part of a leadership development program that had been custom-developed for one company, Jim also designed the exercise to deliver on the broader program goal of network and colleague development.

The morning began with an interactive discussion of product life cycles and how organizational culture and leaders evolve as products succeed and organizations grow. This was followed by an exploration of the unique types of innovation: process, sustaining (incremental), and disruptive (new growth).

At this point, Jim used Leadership Metaphor Explorer to help identify the leadership behaviors and cultural attributes that had been hinted at during the morning's discussion. First, he asked each group to discuss messages from the 15 cards at their table and then collaborate to select up to four cards that depict leadership behaviors or cultural attributes that disable innovation. They were asked to share

- the disabling behaviors or cultural characteristics they saw in the image
- the type or types of innovation that would be inhibited
- the ways in which leaders display such disabling behaviors or organizational culture works to send out these subtle messages

A sampling of cards and comments selected during this round included

- Calculating Brains—force outcomes based on the needs of now
- Well-Defended Warriors—use power to overcome resistance, oblivious to outside intelligence
- Swarm of Bees—what happens to people in our company if they make a mistake or fall short

Next, Jim asked each group to revisit its discussions and collaborate to select up to four cards that depict leadership behaviors or cultural attributes that enable innovation. This time, they were asked to share

- the connections between the images and the enabling behaviors or cultural characteristics
- the type or types of innovation that would be supported
- the ways in which leaders display and cultures support such enabling behaviors

A sampling of cards and comments selected during this round included

- Shepherd—guiding, protective against interference, observant and listening, comes in all sizes and types

Amabile & Center for Creative Leadership. *KEYS to creativity and innovation.*

Association for Managers of Innovation.

Center for Creative Leadership & Continuum. Innovation leadership.

Gryskiewicz. *Positive turbulence.*

Gryskiewicz & Taylor. *Making creativity practical.*

Horth & Buchner. *Innovation leadership.*

Palus & Horth. *The leader's edge.*

Rosenfeld. *The essence of innovation.*

- Cocreating Musicians—teams of unique contributors working in a highly integrated way to deliver a success they could not deliver individually
- Garage of Innovators—an overall favorite card among all the participants

The following four cards were used to tell one story: Polarity of Opposites coming together, with the help of involved, knowledgeable Player-Coaches, can organize and integrate a Community of (diverse) Craftspeople to set sail together as Ambitious Pioneers charting a new course.

Each table captured its key messages from the cards and the discussions that spontaneously followed, thus enabling the participants to begin building their own vision for innovation leadership. The Leadership Metaphor Explorer experience heightened the awareness of how perspectives differ when viewing the same image or situation.

APPLICATION: LEADERSHIP CULTURE

Culture matters. Culture sets norms on everything in an organization: how to share bad news, whether to take risks, whether and how people are developed and promoted, how people interact with one another, how problems are solved. When people say, "It's just the way things are around here," they're talking about culture (McGuire & Rhodes, 2009).

Where strategy meets culture, culture wins. Organizations seeking to grow and adapt in the face of complex challenges cannot achieve either using only technical approaches such as restructuring and reengineering. Lack of culture development is why 66 to 75 percent of organizational change initiatives fail (McGuire & Rhodes, 2009).

Leadership culture is the self-reinforcing web of individual and collective beliefs and practices in a collective (group, organization, community) that produce the outcomes of shared direction, alignment, and commitment. Beliefs unconsciously drive decisions and behaviors, and repeated behaviors become leadership practices (Drath, Palus, & McGuire, 2010; Palus, McGuire, & Ernst, 2011).

Benefits of This Application

- Creates shared understanding about the challenges at hand
- Creates fresh, memorable metaphors and stories about a complex challenge that engage people in finding solutions
- Builds safety for self-disclosure and vulnerability
- Improves interpersonal understanding and trust
- Elicits new questions and alternatives
- Helps people envision a better future
- Helps people see their environment and their organization with fresh eyes
- Legitimizes intuition and emotion
- Encourages fun, playful, yet serious dialogue
- Spans boundaries, contexts, and cultures
- Produces tangible images that can be reused in paper and digital forms

There are three main types of leadership culture: dependent, independent, and interdependent.

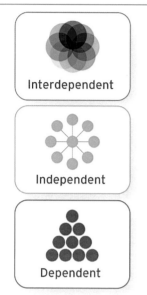

Leadership is a **collective** activity.

Leadership emerges out of **individual knowledge and expertise.**

People in authority are responsible for leadership.

Figure 10. Three leadership types.

Facilitation

The basic instructions for Leadership Metaphor Explorer apply. The facilitator needs to have experience and skill commensurate with the group and situation. Participants should first be introduced to the topic of leadership culture in a manner relevant to their situation. Transforming leadership culture requires more than Leadership Metaphor Explorer sessions.

Example of This Application in Action

During an advanced management course at Virginia Tech, Tom Hickok used Leadership Metaphor Explorer in a joint session with 15 students in two locations. The students represented a mix of U.S. local and federal organizations. Part of the purpose of the joint session was to build community between the two groups of students.

Tom started the session by letting the students know that the day's discussion would be followed by an exercise. The discussion began with the class brainstorming a number of characteristics of high-performing organizations. Then the class chose one of those characteristics, accountability, and talked about what the term meant operationally—that is, how one would implement it, what the consequences of failure to implement it might be, and how it could be measured.

Next, Tom laid out the Leadership Metaphor Explorer cards on several tables and asked the students to pick one or two cards that spoke to them in respect to the accountability challenges facing a high-performing organization. Students chose a card or cards from either a negative (an obstacle to achieving accountability) or positive (a way to achieve accountability) perspective. The students knew they would talk about their choices later in the class.

Examples of the Leadership Metaphor Explorer cards students chose and discussed include

- Strict Disciplinarians—how rules can stifle creativity
- Cocreating Musicians—high performance as improvisational jazz
- Squadron of Jet Fighters—the need for executive training to simulate real situations
- Union of Independent States—new stovepipes, or silos, replacing old ones

The ensuing discussion provoked some instances of self-disclosure and several insights into the students' respective organizations. Students recognized the power of dialogue to create unity among them, and they expressed how Leadership Metaphor Explorer encouraged them to see the class as a safe place for what otherwise might be difficult conversations.

Additional Resources for This Application

Drath. *The deep blue sea.*

Drath, Palus, & McGuire. Developing interdependent leadership.

McCauley, Drath, Palus, O'Connor, & Baker. The use of constructive-developmental theory to advance the understanding of leadership.

McCauley, Palus, Drath, Hughes, McGuire, O'Connor, & Van Velsor. *Interdependent leadership in organizations.*

McGuire & Rhodes. *Transforming your leadership culture.*

Palus. A declaration of interdependence.

Quinn & Van Velsor. Developing globally responsible leadership.

APPLICATION: TALENT MANAGEMENT

Talent management defines an organization's efforts to attract, develop, and retain skilled, valuable employees. Through that effort, the organization strives to select and develop people with the capabilities and commitment needed for current and future organizational success (Campbell & Smith, 2010).

Facilitation

The basic instructions for Leadership Metaphor Explorer apply. The facilitator should have experience and skill commensurate with the group and situation.

Example of This Application in Action

Greg Laskow, a senior faculty member at CCL, used Leadership Metaphor Explorer with representatives from multiple federal agencies

Benefits of This Application

- Creates shared understanding about the challenges at hand
- Builds safety for self-disclosure and vulnerability
- Improves interpersonal understanding and trust
- Elicits new questions and alternatives
- Helps people envision a better future
- Helps people see their environment and their organization with fresh eyes
- Legitimizes intuition and emotion
- Generates alternative futures for wiser planning
- Encourages fun, playful, yet serious dialogue
- Taps into personal experiences and passions
- Surfaces individual and group assumptions
- Spans boundaries, contexts, and cultures
- Produces tangible images that can be reused in paper and digital forms
- Helps people move from ineffective positions

Berke, Kossler, & Wakefield. *Developing leadership talent.*

Campbell & Criswell. *The pillars of successful executive leadership.*

Campbell & Smith. *High-potential talent.*

Kaiser. *Filling the leadership pipeline.*

Sessa & Taylor. *Executive selection.*

Smith & Campbell. *Talent conversations.*

during a conference sponsored by CCL and the National Academy of Public Administration. First, he asked participants to write down adjectives in response to the following framing question: In your agency today, how would you describe the talent pool for future leaders?

Next, participants selected one or two Leadership Metaphor Explorer cards that represented the current state of affairs they had described. They then shared with each other the adjectives they had recorded at the start of the session and explained why they made their particular card selections. When Greg asked participants to describe the outcome of their conversations, several participants expressed surprise that they were able to describe their situation in such a short period of time.

APPLICATION: BOUNDARY SPANNING

Every organization has its own particular form of leadership culture that achieves outcomes of direction, alignment, and commitment. Beliefs and practices for achieving direction, alignment, and commitment vary across leadership cultures and subcultures, forming social boundaries of differing beliefs and practices that can block collaborative work (Drath et al., 2008). The successful spanning of these boundaries can lead to more productive work and new frontiers for innovation (Ernst & Chrobot-Mason, 2010).

Benefits of This Application

- Creates shared understanding about the challenges at hand
- Creates fresh, memorable metaphors and stories about a complex challenge that engage people in finding solutions
- Builds safety for self-disclosure and vulnerability
- Improves interpersonal understanding and trust
- Elicits new questions and alternatives
- Helps people envision a better future
- Helps people see their environment and their organization with fresh eyes
- Legitimizes intuition and emotion
- Generates alternative futures for wiser planning
- Encourages fun, playful, yet serious dialogue
- Taps into personal experiences and passions
- Makes abstract conversations tangible
- Frames and illustrates thoughts so they can be shared
- Surfaces individual and group assumptions
- Spans boundaries, contexts, and cultures
- Produces tangible images that can be reused in paper and digital forms
- Helps people move from ineffective positions

Facilitation

Leadership Metaphor Explorer can be used as part of a workshop or retreat aimed at spanning leadership cultures or subcultures. The purpose of the workshop design is to enable two or more different leadership cultures to collaborate on a joint objective by creating shared direction, alignment, and commitment across their boundaries. We refer the reader to the boundary spanning leadership resources at www.spanboundaries .com, including the book *Boundary Spanning Leadership* (Ernst & Chrobot-Mason, 2010), for ideas on creating an effective design for bringing groups together in these ways. Leadership Metaphor Explorer can help when used as a tool for dialogue to identify and explore the cultures themselves, facilitated in much the same way as throughout this guide.

The first option is to have each subgroup present in the room. Each group chooses Leadership Metaphor Explorer cards to describe its own present and future desired leadership culture. Members of each group share these first among themselves. Then the groups present their cards to each other, including reflecting on the specific cards the other group has chosen.

A second option is used when only one group is in the room and the group members want to include their relationships with other groups as part of their strategic thinking. In this case break into groups of six to eight and have each group construct a flip chart matrix with Relationship Now and Relationship Future at the top as column headings, and a list of three to four groups including one's own group at the left as row headings. In dialogue in each small group, fill in the matrix with answers to the question, How do we relate with each group now, and how do we want to relate with each group in the future? With one's own group the question becomes, How do we relate to each other internally within our own group's culture?

Example of This Application in Action

One hundred top managers in a high-tech division were in a retreat receiving a new strategic direction. A key focus was about how they would enact and "partner" the strategy with better coordination and collaboration with other divisions and groups in the same organization. Each partner was unique in terms of its cultural beliefs and practices.

We divided the managers into groups of six to eight. Members of work groups within the division were distributed among the groups. Each group was assigned two other divisions or groups, Partner A and Partner B, within the larger organization. Each group also had to think about internal relationships in the division among themselves. Each group was given a deck of Leadership Metaphor Explorer cards and the same instructions and framing questions: How do we need to work together differently to most effectively implement this strategy? What does the relationship between us and Partner A look like now? Between us and Partner B? What will these relationships need to look like in the future to enact our strategy? What will the relationships among the clusters in our division need to look like?

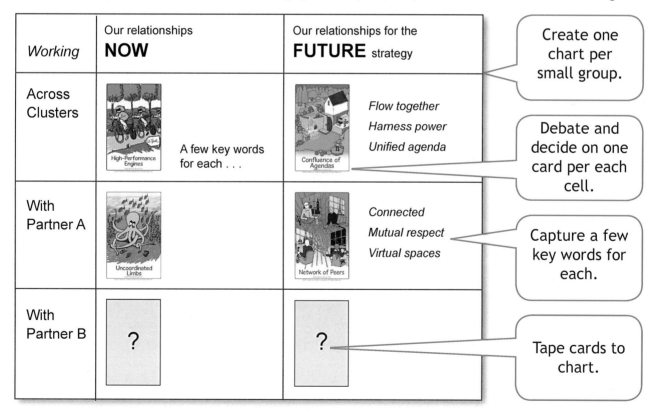

Figure 11. Instructions given to participants.

Ernst & Chrobot-Mason. *Boundary spanning leadership.*

Ernst & Yip. Boundary spanning leadership.

Hughes, Palus, Ernst, Houston, & McGuire. Boundary spanning across
leadership cultures.

Each person chose a Leadership Metaphor Explorer card for each
cell in the matrix. Each group then decided on the card that best represented each of its cells and prepared to share with the large group. Each
group then reported on its response to the question, What themes did we
hear about how we need to operate differently with other groups?

APPLICATION: SCENARIO CREATION

According to Kees van der Heijden (2005), scenarios are plausible stories of the future. Scenario creation is a powerful leadership tool used to navigate through complexity and uncertainty toward a desired future. Leadership Metaphor Explorer can help people create the rich plotlines that make these stories memorable. The resulting collages become a focal point for a conversation that is rich in metaphors and insights. The accompanying dialogue is grounded in serious yet playful inquiry.

Facilitation

By exploring multiple scenarios, groups can map the landscape of possible futures in multiple dimensions and directions. Each scenario outline contains the possible outcomes of the trends and forces that will drive the critical uncertainties in your situation. Each scenario is then named in a way that begins to frame a specific and detailed narrative. At this point you and your team can begin developing a narrative for each scenario as follows:

Benefits of This Application

- Generates alternative futures for wiser planning
- Encourages fun, playful, yet serious dialogue
- Taps into personal experiences and passions
- Makes abstract conversations tangible
- Frames and illustrates thoughts so they can be shared
- Surfaces individual and group assumptions
- Spans boundaries, contexts, and cultures
- Creates fresh, memorable metaphors and stories about a complex challenge that engage people in finding solutions
- Produces tangible images that can be reused in paper and digital forms
- Helps people move from ineffective positions

1. Hang a large sheet of roll paper on the wall so that the narrative can be graphically recorded and facilitated as the group works.

2. Choose one scenario to work with and set the others aside for now; alternatively, assign different scenarios to different teams.

3. Each team talks through its outline so that the group as a whole grasps the various components of the scenario.

4. Explore what this future might look like.

   a. Lay out a set of Visual Explorer cards.

   b. Ask each person to silently peruse all of the cards, looking for the one that best describes this scenario's future state as he or she sees it.

   c. Once all have picked a card, invite each person to show his or her selected card, describe what's on the card, and give a rationale for selecting it.

   d. As people present, record their comments on sticky notes. Add their cards and comments to the wall as each finishes presenting.

   e. When all cards have been shared, the entire group talks through the collection and identifies major themes.

5. Determine the actors (people, entities, environment, and so on) and the behaviors that will create this future state.

   a. Lay out a set of Leadership Metaphor Explorer cards.

   b. Ask each person to silently browse all of the cards, looking for those that describe or call to mind an actor and behavior that would help cause this future state.

   c. Once all have picked cards, invite each person to show what he or she selected, describe what the card depicts, and explain the rationale for the selection.

   d. As people present, record their comments on sticky notes. Add their cards and comments to the wall as each finishes presenting.

6. Develop the headline events that will occur as you move from the present to this future state.

a. Give each member of the team a template made from letter-size or A4-size paper.

    i. Divide the paper into three sections, top to bottom.

    ii. At the top of each section is printed the banner of a news-paper, as follows: a local paper, a regional paper, a national paper.

b. Ask each person to write a headline that would appear in each of these newspapers as this future unfolds, considering all of the information produced so far.

c. Have each person cut his or her sheet into three separate head-lines and stick all of them up on the wall.

d. Across your large sheet of paper, draw a timeline that represents the years over which your scenario will develop, beginning with today.

7. Teams can develop a timeline using the following steps:

a. Place the headlines on the timeline where the team expects the event to occur.

b. Add the Leadership Metaphor Explorer cards and include notes as appropriate.

c. Create additional headlines as needed.

d. Look for the emerging narrative.

8. Complete the narrative.

a. By now each team has developed a storyboard—even if it looks more like a collage. Teams can add additional notes, graphics, or other elements as needed to fill out the narrative. Don't worry about the storyboards getting messy; let the action flow in creat-ing the storyboard.

b. The work is done when a member of the team can stand before the finished graphic and use it to tell the complete story of this particular future.

c. Some facilitators like to record a video of the summaries. If you don't videorecord, be sure to photograph everything on the wall when all the teams have finished their summaries. At that point, the graphic representation can be transcribed into a written narrative.

9. Use the scenarios (storyboards plus narratives) to conduct dialogue sessions with other groups throughout the organization and, if relevant, with the community of which the organization is a part. Encourage participants to extend the scenarios into a call for action and to implement what's necessary to achieve the timelines they have created.

Example of This Application in Action

In eastern North Carolina, healthcare reform requirements are robust, but the economy is chronically weak and there is no government funding support for the legislation. Regardless, thousands of new patients are entering the system. At the Brody School of Medicine (BSOM), the director of strategy and planning was looking for a different way to establish a vision for the hospital that met its mission and also accounted for the changes brought about by the Affordable Care Act of 2010.

Additional Resources for This Application

Beatty & Byington. Developing strategic leadership.

de Geus. Strategy and learning.

Flye. The land that time forgot.

Hughes & Beatty. *Becoming a strategic leader.*

Johansen. *Leaders make the future.*

Mieszkowski. Wild cards.

Palus, Horth, Pulley, & Selvin. Exploration for development.

Peterson. *Out of the blue.*

Schwartz. *The art of the long view.*

van der Heijden. *Scenarios.*

Van Velsor. *Youth leadership summit 2011.*

Because circumstances change so rapidly and the future is uncertain, the director decided on a scenario-building approach. To assure relevance in the scenarios, the project began with one-on-one interviews of 26 of the leaders in the BSOM community: faculty, chairs, administrators, board members, and hospital executives. The issues facing the hospital reported in the interviews were organized by theme, and those issues became the frame for scenario building.

To assemble the scenario-building team, the school's dean invited 25 people who represented a cross-section of the school. The team divided into small groups and worked with the 11 themes that emerged from the interviews to derive "critical uncertainties" any scenario should take into account. The small groups used a process whereby they first developed an end state—a vision of the future—and then crafted a narrative about how that future would come about. A videographer captured the stories as they were presented.

Combining Leadership Metaphor Explorer and Visual Explorer

Leadership Metaphor Explorer works well in combination with another CCL tool, Visual Explorer, which is particularly effective in deepening dialogue and exploring challenges.

Discovery to Action

Our colleague and master explorer Hamish Taylor at Shinergise offers the following discovery-to-action model for group performance, combining Leadership Metaphor Explorer and Visual Explorer:

> I still find Visual Explorer is the more versatile tool for exploration, though undoubtedly Leadership Metaphor Explorer is more powerful as a diagnostic for change management without needing as much conceptual interpretation. In fact, what I find particularly helpful is to integrate several approaches into a sequenced discovery-to-action model.
>
> First, we use Visual Explorer in Thematic Cluster mode, either individually (repeated if necessary with different people) or in a team syndicate session. This surfaces critical themes and allows for prioritization of the issues and challenges facing a group.
>
> Then we use Leadership Metaphor Explorer in Thematic Cluster mode, often run in a Best of Us – Us under Pressure filter mode, which surfaces good and bad behavior. This is particularly effective when you use partner pairs who have an in-depth dialogue with each other before returning to the table for a team sharing session, in which the pairs place their cards on the table and look at the overall patterns.
>
> Then we use Visual Explorer again in single-image Star Model mode. The discovery and surfacing process now allows going deep on a single dimension or approaching the problem from a particular perspective and then opening up the dialogue to new routes to resolution.

Future Scenarios

This case, using Visual Explorer and Leadership Metaphor Explorer for future scenarios, is from Bruce Flye's work (see more on this case in the Leadership Strategy Application on page 45).

Bruce describes the process:

> First, they used Visual Explorer to develop the end state of a particular scenario. You can see a 10-minute video of their descriptions at https://sites.google.com/site/strategicconversationsatbsom/home/the-bsom-scenarios/scenarios-workshop-3.
>
> Next, I had them use Leadership Metaphor Explorer to determine the characters that would take us from now to the end states. Cards were picked quickly—no hesitation—and the subsequent conversation was incredibly rich.
>
> Finally, they came up with the headlines that the characters would generate over the next five years. They were given 40 minutes to get all of that into a narrative form.
>
> So how do you go from cards and cutouts to a written narrative with physicians and scientists? My bright idea was to have a legitimate videographer come in. It was amazing how a camera seemed to turn these guys into Walter Cronkites. There were interesting shifts in perspectives. The narratives did not go quite as anyone expected, and there was a new awareness in the room. Leadership Metaphor Explorer and Visual Explorer seemed to grease the conversations, quickly opening up a lot of complexity that avoided obvious outcomes.

Mental Models

David Horth shares this example of using Leadership Metaphor Explorer with Visual Explorer when working with a group on mental models of leadership—that is, how we define leadership, what we believe leadership to be. These models can be personal, but they are also part of shared culture. They determine how we enact leadership and how we respond to the leadership of others. They are often implicit rather than explicit. Being aware of our models is important so that we can live up to them and develop new models for new challenges.

David was working with a group of 50 executives from a government agency. His objective was to get them all to be aware and reflect together on their mental models of leadership, and how those models might be affecting their approach to their complex challenges. The following is the process he used.

1. First, ask the whole group these questions:
   - Why is leadership important?
   - What's going on in your world that calls for leadership?
   - What's going on that calls for creativity?
   - What are you like when you are most effective as a leader?

2. Split up into small groups to discuss the questions. Capture on a flip chart a single-word or short-phrase response to each of these questions from each small group.

3. Ask the whole group why they were asked these questions. Typically they get to a response like "to see where we were coming from." Rephrase this as "probing to discover our mental models of leadership, how we think about leadership."

4. Give a brief lecture on leadership and creativity.

5. Give each small group a set of Visual Explorer cards, a set of Leadership Metaphor Explorer cards, and these directions:
   - Choose a Visual Explorer image related to your complex challenge.
   - Choose one Leadership Metaphor Explorer card that speaks to your leadership now and one that speaks to the leadership you need to move this challenge forward.
   - Dialogue about the images and metaphors. You can use the Star Model (found in the Visual Explorer Facilitator Guide) for mediated dialogue.

6. Arrange the cards on a table, ranging from Now to Desired Future.

7. Debrief in plenary session.

8. Give a brief lecture on stages of personal and cultural development: dependent to independent to interdependent. These are the sources of our models ("action logics"). See "Seven Transformations of Leadership" (Rooke & Torbert, 2005).

9. Discuss further and close.

Skills for Contemporary Leadership

David Horth provides this field report on using Leadership Metaphor Explorer and Visual Explorer to address skills for contemporary leadership: "The following design was used successfully at the Library Leadership and Management Association presidents' meeting in June 2008 in Anaheim, California. I was expecting about 10 people, but more like 300 people came, so I had to think quickly on my feet." The following is the process he used.

1. Put one Leadership Metaphor Explorer card and one Visual Explorer card facedown on each chair, randomly distributed.

2. Open the session with the question: How does the Leadership Metaphor Explorer card you have been assigned describe leadership in your organization in any one of these ways?
   - in the past
   - when your organization is at its worst
   - as currently practiced
   - when your organization is at its best
   - that you would like in the future
   - needed to resolve your most pressing challenges

3. Ask participants to discuss their answers with their neighbors.

4. Invite people to come to the microphone with the card they received to share what they had found. (This was very rich. About seven people came forward before I moved on to the next part of the session. They shared the metaphor and the insights they had gained.)

5. Use Leadership Metaphor Explorer cards to talk about how we think leadership will look in the future (see Figure 12, page 70).

Honorable Captains

Adventuresome Explorers

Leaderless Orchestra

Figure 12. Dependent leadership illustrated by Honorable Captains, independent by Adventuresome Explorers, and interdependent by Leaderless Orchestra.

6. Present the Sense-Making Loop (Palus & Horth, 2002, p. 6) used as a response to complex challenges.

7. Ask each person to look at the Visual Explorer card he or she received and to think of a complex challenge in his or her organization. Ask this question: How does the visual image you have been assigned describe your complex challenge?

8. Ask people to come up to the microphone to share insights on the process and what they have learned.

References and Resources

Ackoff, R. L., Magidson, J., & Addison, H. J. (2006). *Idealized design: How to dissolve tomorrow's crisis . . . today.* Philadelphia, PA: Wharton School Publishing.

Amabile, T., & Center for Creative Leadership. (2010). *KEYS to creativity and innovation.* Minnetonka, MN: Data Solutions. Information at http://www.ccl.org/leadership/assessments/KEYSOverview.aspx

Association for Managers of Innovation (AMI). Access at http://www.ccl.org/ leadership/community/ami/index.aspx

Beatty, K. C., & Byington, B. (2010). Developing strategic leadership. In E. Van Velsor, C. D. McCauley, & M. N. Ruderman (Eds.), *The Center for Creative Leadership handbook of leadership development* (3rd ed., pp. 313–334). San Francisco, CA: Jossey-Bass.

Berke, D., Kossler, M. E., & Wakefield, M. (2008). *Developing leadership talent.* Hoboken, NJ: Wiley.

Campbell, M., & Criswell, C. (Presenters). (2007, September 18). *The pillars of successful executive leadership: What we know about senior leaders and what it means for your development* [Web presentation]. Greensboro, NC: Center for Creative Leadership. Retrieved from http://www.ccl.org/leadership/community/pillarsWebinar.aspx

Campbell, M., & Smith, R. (2010). *High-potential talent: A view from inside the leadership pipeline* [White paper]. Greensboro, NC: Center for Creative Leadership. Retrieved from http://www.ccl.org/leadership/pdf/research/highPotentialTalent.pdf

Center for Creative Leadership & Continuum. (2012). Innovation leadership [Workshop]. Information at http://www.ccl.org/leadership/programs/ILWOverview.aspx

de Geus, A. (1999). Strategy and learning. *Reflections, 1*(1), 75–81.

Dennett, D. C. (1991). *Consciousness explained.* Boston, MA: Little, Brown & Company.

Drath, W. H. (2001). *The deep blue sea: Rethinking the source of leadership.* San Francisco, CA: Jossey-Bass.

Drath, W. H., McCauley, C. D., Palus, C. J., Van Velsor, E., O'Connor, P. M. G., & McGuire, J. B. (2008). Direction, alignment, commitment: Toward a more integrative ontology of leadership. *Leadership Quarterly, 19,* 635–653.

Drath, W. H., Palus, C. J., & McGuire, J. B. (2010). Developing interdependent leadership. In E. Van Velsor, C. D. McCauley, & M. N. Ruderman (Eds.), *The Center for Creative Leadership handbook of leadership development* (3rd ed., pp. 405–428). San Francisco, CA: Jossey-Bass.

Ernst, C., & Chrobot-Mason, D. (2010). *Boundary spanning leadership: Six practices for solving problems, driving innovation, and transforming organizations.* New York, NY: McGraw-Hill.

Ernst, C., & Yip, J. (2009). Boundary spanning leadership: Tactics to bridge social identity groups in organizations. In T. L. Pittinsky (Ed.), *Crossing the divide: Intergroup leadership in a world of difference* (pp. 89–99). Boston, MA: Harvard Business School Press.

Flye, B. (2012, January 3). The land that time forgot [Web log post]. Retrieved from http://makingvoicesvisible.blogspot.com/2012/01/bsom-scenario-3-land-that-time-forgot.html

Frankovelgia, C., & Martineau, J. (2006). Coaching teams. In S. Ting & P. Scisco (Eds.), *The CCL handbook of coaching: A guide for the leader coach* (pp. 379–403). San Francisco, CA: Jossey-Bass.

Gryskiewicz, S. S. (1999). *Positive turbulence: Developing climates for creativity, innovation, and renewal.* San Francisco, CA: Jossey-Bass.

Gryskiewicz, S. S., & Taylor, S. (2003). *Making creativity practical: Innovation that gets results.* Greensboro, NC: Center for Creative Leadership.

Horth, D., & Buchner, D. (2009). *Innovation leadership: How to use innovation to lead effectively, work collaboratively and drive results* [White paper]. Greensboro, NC: Center for Creative Leadership. Retrieved from http://www.ccl.org/leadership/pdf/research/InnovationLeadership.pdf

Hughes, R. L., & Beatty, K. C. (2005). *Becoming a strategic leader: Your role in your organization's enduring success.* San Francisco, CA: Jossey-Bass.

Hughes, R., Ginnett, R., & Curphy, G. (2011). *Leadership: Enhancing the lessons of experience* (7th ed.). New York, NY: McGraw-Hill.

Hughes, R. L., Palus, C. J., Ernst, C., Houston, G. G., & McGuire, J. B. (2011). Boundary spanning across leadership cultures: A leadership strategy for the comprehensive approach. In D. J. Neil & L. Wells II (Eds.), *Capability development in support of comprehensive approaches: Transforming international civil-military interactions* (pp. 125–141).Washington, DC: National Defense University Press.

Jaynes, J. (1976). *The origin of consciousness in the breakdown of the bicameral mind.* Boston, MA: Houghton Mifflin.

Johansen, B. (2012). *Leaders make the future: Ten new leadership skills for an uncertain world* (2nd ed.). San Francisco, CA: Berrett-Koehler.

Kaiser, R. B. (2005). *Filling the leadership pipeline.* Greensboro, NC: Center for Creative Leadership.

Kegan, R. (1994). *In over our heads: The mental demands of modern life.* Cambridge, MA: Harvard University Press.

King, S. N., & Altman, D. (2011). *Discovering the leader in you workbook.* San Francisco, CA: Jossey-Bass.

King, S. N., Altman, D., & Lee, R. J. (2011). *Discovering the leader in you: How to realize your leadership potential.* San Francisco, CA: Jossey-Bass.

Lakoff, G., & Johnson, M. (2003). *Metaphors we live by* (2nd ed.). Chicago, IL: University of Chicago Press.

Mair, J. M. M. (1977). Metaphors for living. In A. W. Landfield (Ed.), *Nebraska symposium on motivation, 1976* (pp. 243–290). Lincoln, NE: University of Nebraska Press.

McAdams, D. P. (1997). *The stories we live by: Personal myths and the making of the self.* New York, NY: Guilford Press.

McCauley, C. (2011). *Making leadership happen* [White paper]. Greensboro, NC: Center for Creative Leadership. Retrieved from http://www.ccl.org/leadership/pdf/research/MakingLeadershipHappen.pdf

McCauley, C. D., Drath, W. H., Palus, C. J., O'Connor, P. M. G., & Baker, B. A. (2006). The use of constructive-developmental theory to advance the understanding of leadership. *Leadership Quarterly, 17*, 634–653.

McCauley, C. D., Palus, C. J., Drath, W. H., Hughes, R. L., McGuire, J. B., O'Connor, P. M. G., & Van Velsor, E. (2008). *Interdependent leadership in organizations: Evidence from six case studies.* Greensboro, NC: Center for Creative Leadership.

McGuire, J. B., Palus, C. J., Pasmore, W., & Rhodes, G. (2009). *Transforming your organization* [White paper]. Greensboro, NC: Center for Creative Leadership. Retrieved from http://www.ccl.org/leadership/pdf/solutions/TYO.pdf

McGuire, J. B., & Rhodes, G. (2009). *Transforming your leadership culture.* San Francisco, CA: Jossey-Bass.

Mieszkowski, K. (1998, February). Wild cards: Report from the futurist. *Fast Company, 13*, 30.

O'Neil, J., & Marsick, V. J. (2007). *Understanding action learning.* New York, NY: AMACOM.

Ospina, S., & Foldy, E. (2010). Building bridges from the margins: The work of leadership in social change organizations. *Leadership Quarterly, 21*(2), 292–307.

Palus, C. (2009, July 13). How can leadership be taught: Symposium at the Harvard Business School. Retrieved from http://www.cclexplorer.org/2009/visualexplorer/how-can-leadership-be-taught-symposium-at-the-harvard-business-school

Palus, C. J. (2010, June 3). A declaration of interdependence [Web log post]. Retrieved from http://blogs.hbr.org/imagining-the-future-of-leadership/2010/06/a-declaration-of-interdependen.html

Palus, C. J., & Drath, W. H. (2001). Putting something in the middle: An approach to dialogue. *Reflections, 3*(2), 28–39.

Palus, C. J., & Horth, D. M. (2002). *The leader's edge: Six creative competencies for navigating complex challenges.* San Francisco, CA: Jossey-Bass.

Palus, C. J., Horth, D. M., Pulley, M. L., & Selvin, A. M. (2003). Exploration for development: Developing leadership by making shared sense of complex challenges. *Consulting Psychology Journal, 55*(1), 26–40.

Palus, C. J., McGuire, J. B., & Ernst, C. (2011). Developing interdependent leadership. In S. Snook, N. Nohria, & R. Khurana (Eds.), *The handbook for teaching leadership* (pp. 467–492). Thousand Oaks, CA: Sage Publications.

Palus, C. J., McGuire, J. B., & Rhodes, G. B. (2010). Evolving your leadership culture. In D. L. Dotlich, P. C. Cairo, & S. H. Rhinesmith (Eds.), *2010 Pfeiffer annual: Leadership development* (pp. 185–195). San Francisco, CA: Pfeiffer.

Pasmore, B., & Lafferty, K. (2009). *Developing a leadership strategy: A critical ingredient for organizational success* [White paper]. Greensboro, NC: Center for Creative Leadership. Retrieved from http://www.ccl.org/leadership/pdf/research/LeadershipStrategy.pdf

Peterson, J. L. (1999). *Out of the blue: How to anticipate big future surprises* (2nd ed.). Lanham, MD: Madison Books.

Quinn, L., & Van Velsor, E. (2010). Developing globally responsible leadership. In E. Van Velsor, C. D. McCauley, & M. N. Ruderman (Eds.), *The Center for Creative Leadership handbook of leadership development* (3rd ed., pp. 345–374). San Francisco, CA: Jossey-Bass.

Rimanoczy, R., & Turner, E. (2008). *Action reflection learning: Solving real business problems by connecting learning with earning.* Boston, MA: Nicholas Brealey Publishing.

Rooke, D., & Torbert, W. R. (2005). Seven transformations of leadership. *Harvard Business Review, 83*(4), 66–76.

Rosenfeld, B. *The essence of innovation: 5 principles* [Podcast]. Retrieved from http://www.ccl.org/leadership/podcast/transcript5Principles.aspx

Schwartz, P. (1991). *The art of the long view.* New York, NY: Doubleday.

Sessa, V. L., & Taylor, J. J. (2000). *Executive selection: Strategies for success.* San Francisco, CA: Jossey-Bass.

Sewerin, T. (2009). *Leadership, teams and coaching.* Malmo, Sweden: Tertulia Books.

Smith, R., & Campbell, M. (2011). *Talent conversations: What they are, why they're crucial, and how to do them right.* Greensboro, NC: Center for Creative Leadership.

Ting, S., & Riddle, D. (2006). A framework for leadership development coaching. In S. Ting & P. Scisco (Eds.), *The CCL handbook of coaching: A guide for the leader coach* (pp. 34–62). San Francisco, CA: Jossey-Bass.

Torbert, B., & Associates. (2004). *Action inquiry: The secret of timely and transforming leadership.* San Francisco, CA: Berrett-Koehler.

van der Heijden, K. (2005). *Scenarios: The art of strategic conversation* (2nd ed.). New York, NY: Wiley.

Van Velsor, E. (2011). *Youth leadership summit 2011: Creating community, finding one voice: Reflections & insights* [White paper]. Greensboro, NC: Center for Creative Leadership. Retrieved from http://www.ccl.org/leadership/pdf/research/YouthLeadershipSummit.pdf

Van Velsor, E., McCauley, C. D., & Ruderman, M. N. (Eds.). (2010). *The Center for Creative Leadership handbook of leadership development* (3rd ed.). San Francisco, CA: Jossey-Bass.

Whyte, D. (2002). *Crossing the unknown sea: Work as a pilgrimage of identity.* New York, NY: Riverhead Trade.

Wilber, K. (2000). *Integral psychology.* Boston, MA: Shambala.

Frequently Asked Questions

Q **Who can conduct a Leadership Metaphor Explorer session? Will I be able to conduct the Leadership Metaphor Explorer session by myself? What if I lack experience?**

A Leadership Metaphor Explorer does not necessarily require a trained facilitator. It is often self-facilitated by a leader or member of a team, although most sessions benefit from prior experience and skill at facilitation. Leadership Metaphor Explorer is somewhat self-correcting and forgiving, such that the default process tends to be a positive one—a good conversation supported by meaningful imagery. A Leadership Metaphor Explorer facilitator need only support dialogue among the session participants, which usually requires only a beginner's level of facilitation skill.

- -

Q **Does Leadership Metaphor Explorer really work?**

A Leadership Metaphor Explorer is effective in a wide variety of situations, in part because it's so simple. But its unobtrusiveness and simplicity can be misleading. A dose of skepticism is to be expected and can even prove useful in any process that seeks to question assumptions, as a Leadership Metaphor Explorer session often does. As long as the group's selected topic is relevant and carries a sense of urgency, so that the dialogue is about things that matter most, almost every participant experiences some value from taking part in the Leadership Metaphor Explorer process.

Q What do you tell participants when setting up the exercise?

A You need to address the two main questions the group will have:
- Why are we doing this activity?
- What are the instructions?

Just give a brief, clear rationale based on addressing some shared issue, with Leadership Metaphor Explorer as merely one tool for looking at the issue. Don't position Leadership Metaphor Explorer as some kind of magic bullet. The instruction you give can vary according to the group and the specific application, but you can quickly go over the process at the beginning of the session.

Q What do you tell people who are skeptical of the value of Leadership Metaphor Explorer?

A We actually invite people to be skeptical, but we also invite them to hold their skepticism lightly and enter the experience "as if it made sense." Usually, it soon does, as the conversation deepens.

Q Is Leadership Metaphor Explorer a game, or is it a simulation?

A Leadership Metaphor Explorer is not in itself a team exercise, game, or simulation. There is no single right way to use it. It's a flexible tool used to facilitate a good conversation.

Q **I work with executives. They don't like this touchy-feely stuff. How will Leadership Metaphor Explorer work with them?**

A Because Leadership Metaphor Explorer is not an exercise but adapts to the purposes at hand, it takes on a serious feel when used in these kinds of situations. Leadership Metaphor Explorer has worked well with all kinds of senior leader audiences, including military leaders and chief financial officers (the serious kind).

Q **How much space does it require?**

A It works very nicely to have a separate room to lay out the images so they can be comfortably browsed, especially if the group size is more than 20. On the other hand, Leadership Metaphor Explorer is extremely portable. The cards can be browsed as a handheld deck or spread on a tabletop.

Q **How much advance planning does a Leadership Metaphor Explorer session require?**

A Those who know Leadership Metaphor Explorer reasonably well can have it as a tool "in their back pocket" with no advance planning whatsoever. More typically, the planning time depends on whether it has been specifically designed into a training program or organizational intervention.

Q How much time is needed to conduct a Leadership Metaphor Explorer session?

A The session itself can be done in less than an hour. Groups sometimes extend the dialogue productively for hours and hours.

Q What do the metaphors mean?

A See pages 79–85.

What Do the Metaphors Mean?

Do not distribute the following list to participants; it's meant only for your reference as a facilitator. When participants ask what a metaphor means, we often reply (in a sincere tone), "What do *you* think it might mean?" The following descriptions should not replace any of the participants' interpretations.

Metaphor	Explanation
Adventuresome Explorers	Adventuresome Explorers risk danger as they seek and explore new places and new ideas.
Ambitious Pioneers	Ambitious Pioneers are among the first ones into a new place or a new way of thinking.
Autonomous Teammates	Autonomous Teammates are on the same team but think and act independently.
Battle-Hardened Soldiers	Battle-Hardened Soldiers have been through great struggles and are stronger because of it.
Beasts of Burden	Beasts of Burden carry their heavy load, day after day.
By-the-Book Commanders	By-the-Book Commanders follow all the rules as they battle forces of man and nature.
Calculating Brains	Calculating Brains analyze the numbers to reach conclusions
Cave Dwellers	Cave Dwellers live in the past and ignore recent innovations.
Circle of Inclusion	A Circle of Inclusion welcomes all people to a peaceful dialogue.

Metaphor	Explanation
Coalition of Enemies	A Coalition of Enemies unites across deep differences to face a common threat across boundaries.
Cocreating Musicians	Cocreating Musicians make music with harmonies as well as with differences and discord.
Colonial Rulers	Colonial Rulers are the arrogant bosses of conquered land.
Colony of Artists	A Colony of Artists blends unique talents into a single school of art.
Community of Craftspeople	A Community of Craftspeople builds great things together.
Community of Practice	A Community of Practice focuses on doing one thing well together as a learning community.
Community of Strangers	A Community of Strangers lives together without really knowing each other.
Conflict Smoother	A Conflict Smoother tries to hide disagreements and make things look smooth.
Confluence of Agendas	A Confluence of Agendas combines different pathways into one common goal.
Connected Leadership	Connected Leadership builds shared direction, alignment, and commitment across boundaries in an interdependent world.
Conquering Generals	Conquering Generals must be peacemakers.
Constellation of Stars	A Constellation of Stars brings wise people together in a new relationship.

Metaphor	Explanation
Council of Elders	A Council of Elders consists of those who share power and authority in a community in which age is respected.
Courageous Lion Tamers	Courageous Lion Tamers crack the whip and gain obedience from wild animals.
Creative Troubleshooters	Creative Troubleshooters can fix anything for anyone.
Critical Parents	Critical Parents are harsh and demanding to others, whom they treat as children.
Death-Defying Tightrope Walkers	Death-Defying Tightrope Walkers are brave and take great risks, to great applause—but they act alone.
Dependable Repairmen	Dependable Repairmen show up and do the work in any conditions, rain or sunshine.
Dynamic Ecosystem	A Dynamic Ecosystem supports mutual adaptation in a shared ecology.
Enlightened Gurus	Enlightened Gurus have followers who sit at their feet to be taught.
Entertaining Ringleader	An Entertaining Ringleader brings forth all the acts in a circus to the delight of the crowd.
Evangelistic Preachers	Evangelistic Preachers teach their religion to unbelievers as the one way to God.
Fierce Dinosaurs	Fierce Dinosaurs are primitive creatures with sharp claws and teeth.
Garage of Innovators	A Garage of Innovators creates new inventions in a small shed with their friends and families.

Metaphor	Explanation
Geese Flying in Formation	Geese Flying in Formation take turns in front, and get lift from each other's wings.
Greedy Politicians	Greedy Politicians take everything while they kiss babies and make promises.
High-Performance Engines	High-Performance Engines train themselves to excel and cooperate at the highest levels of performance.
Honorable Captains	Honorable Captains take care of the crew and go down with the ship if necessary.
House of Parliament	A House of Parliament unites all the classes of people into a forum for dialogue and decisions.
Interweaving Streams	Interweaving Streams in the same river are only temporarily separate.
Irresponsible Player	An Irresponsible Player denies responsibility for shared work.
King of the Jungle	A King of the Jungle dominates the other beasts with his power.
Leaderless Orchestra	A Leaderless Orchestra makes music by following along with each other.
Micromanagers	Micromanagers try to control every detail of other people's work.
Moneylenders	Moneylenders are greedy for other people's wealth.
Motivational Coaches	Motivational Coaches get the best out of their players.

Metaphor	Explanation
Network of Peers	A Network of Peers is a web of connections among people in similar roles.
Nonviolent Resisters	Nonviolent Resisters follow the principle of nonviolent protest in response to oppression.
Nurturing Parents	Nurturing Parents take care of children who depend on them.
Overbearing Fathers	Overbearing Fathers are never satisfied with the achievements of their children.
Partnership of Equals	A Partnership of Equals is a balance of interests in a committed union.
Peaceful Warriors	Peaceful Warriors bravely serve society around the globe.
Player-Coaches	Player-Coaches play the game and reflect on the game at the same time.
Playground Bully	A Playground Bully is mean to kids.
Polarity of Opposites	A Polarity of Opposites unifies the extremes as a source of energy.
Pool of Sharks	A Pool of Sharks destroys anything weak as a source of food.
Predatory Profiteers	Predatory Profiteers exploit the misfortune of others for personal gain.
Prince of Thieves	A Prince of Thieves has a vision of theft and deceit that others follow.
Resigned Prisoners	Resigned Prisoners don't realize that the door to their cage is open.

Metaphor	Explanation
Roving Musicians	Roving Musicians cross boundaries with their music making.
Ruthless Gang Bosses	Ruthless Gang Bosses leave dead bodies in their war for power.
Self-Catalyzing Renaissance	A Self-Catalyzing Renaissance uses the energy of art and science to create a revolution.
Self-Serving Gold Diggers	Self-Serving Gold Diggers are in it only for themselves.
Shepherd	A Shepherd protects the flock of sheep.
Ship of Fools	A Ship of Fools has no pilot. It carries lost souls ignorant of their own direction.
Silicon Valley of Innovation	A Silicon Valley of Innovation is a community where new ideas and social change are concentrated.
Spoiling Parents	Spoiling Parents hand too much to their children and prevent their growth as people.
Squadron of Jet Fighters	A Squadron of Jet Fighters has the talent and discipline to control powerful machines in a coordinated performance.
Steady Navigators	Steady Navigators continue in the same direction together.
Strict Disciplinarians	Strict Disciplinarians enforce the rules all the time.
Supportive Teachers	Supportive Teachers create a learning environment for eager students.

Metaphor	Explanation
Swarm of Bees	A Swarm of Bees defends its hive without regard for the individual.
Top Dog	A Top Dog is the leader of the pack.
Tyrannical Wardens	Tyrannical Wardens keep the prisoners under control.
Ubuntu—I am because we are	Ubuntu means "I am because we are."
Unassuming Clowns	Unassuming Clowns use humor to bring people together.
Uncoordinated Limbs	Uncoordinated Limbs don't know what the others are doing.
Union of Independent States	A Union of Independent States creates a nation out of competing interests.
Unruly Weeds	Unruly Weeds resist the order of the neat garden.
Visionary Landscapers	Visionary Landscapers imagine a better future from simple beginnings.
Well-Defended Warriors	Well-Defended Warriors defeat their enemies through unity of purpose.
Well Diggers	Well Diggers are experts who can bring prosperity.
Windmill Tilters	Windmill Tilters set out to defeat imaginary enemies, and sometimes win.
World-Class Athletes	World-Class Athletes outrun the competition.

About the Designers

David Magellan Horth is a senior fellow at the Center for Creative Leadership. He is a program designer and an accomplished trainer in a range of custom and open-enrollment programs. He is the coauthor of *The Leader's Edge: Six Creative Competencies for Navigating Complex Challenges*. He holds a B.Sc. (Hons) from the University of Surrey in England.

Charles J. Palus is a senior enterprise associate at the Center for Creative Leadership. He conducts research on interdependent leadership and creates innovations for CCL's organizational leadership practice. He is the coauthor of *The Leader's Edge: Six Creative Competencies for Navigating Complex Challenges*. He received his B.S. in chemical engineering from the Pennsylvania State University and his Ph.D. in adult developmental psychology from Boston College.